THE MOSAIC PROJECT BOOK
GREEK STYLE
KATRINA HALL

INTRODUCING MOSAICS

Mosaic design has often been described as 'painting by numbers' and, however basic a description this might be, it does provide a clue to this art form's key attraction – its accessibility. Mosaics are simply the creation of patterns and pictures from pieces of stone, ceramics, porcelain or glass . . . what could be simpler?

The designs range from very simple to very detailed – both can be beautiful. Start with straightforward designs and, as you gain in confidence, move onto more ambitious projects. Experiment with different materials and designs.

You will soon discover why mosaics have existed as an art form for over 2,000 years – some even date the earliest examples of mosaics back to Ancient Mesopotamia in around 3,000 BC. The combination of their decorative and functional attributes ensured the future of mosaics as a versatile and durable art form that will always have an ageless appeal. All you need to enjoy mosaic design is time, patience and imagination.

MATERIALS

Tesserae (which comes from the Latin word for 'square' and Greek word for 'four') is the name of the pieces used to make mosaics. They come in all manner of shapes and sizes and are supplied on sheets or loose. When storing tesserae, you need to make them easily identifiable, so glass or transparent containers are ideal for loose cubes and clearly labelled boxes work well for flat sheets. All adhesives, cements and additives are best stored in a dry, cool place.

Below is a list of the main materials used in mosaic design. However, there are no rules and mosaicists can use any number of other materials including glass beads, buttons, coins, shells, slate, semi-precious stones and broken household china.

Marble tesserae Available in a natural palette of colours, marble tesserae have either polished or unpolished finishes: the former gives a smooth elegant finish whereas the latter has a more rustic look. Cut marble using a hammer and hardie (bolster blade; see page 4) and protect with a sealant. Pieces are commonly 1.5 x 1.5cm ($\frac{5}{8}$ x $\frac{5}{8}$in).

Vitreous glass Available in a range of colours and palettes, these are relatively cheap and resistant to heat and frost making them ideal for both interior and exterior use. Cut glass using mosaic nippers (see page 4). They are usually supplied in single colour sheets of 2 x 2cm ($\frac{3}{4}$ x $\frac{3}{4}$in) or loose in mixed bags.

Porcelain These are supplied unglazed and are available in a wide range of shades. Suited to both internal and external application, they offer excellent 'slip'-resistant properties even when wet. Use mosaic nippers for cutting (see page 4) and follow the advice of your tile supplier with regard to sealants.

Ceramic These are similar to porcelain tesserae except that they are usually glazed.

Smalti These are made from glass, which are prepared and cut into rectangular strips and then into rectangular tesserae. Smalti reflect light beautifully due to irregularities caused by hand-cut glass surfaces. Sold by the 500g (1lb) or 1kg (2lbs) usually in pieces of 1 x 1.5cm ($\frac{1}{2}$ x $\frac{5}{8}$in), smalti are quite expensive but worth every penny! They can be used internally and externally because they are heat and frost proof. Use a hammer and hardie (bolster blade) to cut smalti.

Gold or silver leaf These tesserae are made when a thin layer of 24-carat gold, or silver, is hammered onto a coloured glass backing and covered with a film of veneer glass. These are then hand cut into tesserae, which can lead to irregularities in sizes and shapes. Either plain or rippled, these should be used sparingly for decorative purposes only because the silver or gold breaks down in excessive conditions, such as extreme heat and frost.

Pebbles or stones Available in a variety of colours, sizes and textures, granite and hard stones are recommended for durability and can be used internally and externally.

Household ceramic tiles These come in a wonderful range of colours and sizes, and are very cheap, which makes experimental cutting affordable. Always check the durability of tiles because certain types are prone to cracking under extreme conditions.

Glass and mirror Use these to add a reflective quality to your mosaics. They are available in large panels from glass shops and some tile suppliers, and should be cut very carefully with a glass cutter.

BASIC TOOLS AND TECHNIQUES

The basic mosaicist tool kit can be very simple and you may have most of this equipment around your home already. If not, visit a hardware store, builders' merchant or tile supplier (see page 32).

1. Hardie Sometimes called a bolster blade, this is used with a hammer for cutting marble and smalti. The hardie (bolster blade) is a small metal block with an anvil-shaped edge, which can either be embedded in concrete in a flower pot or in an upright log.

2. Hammer This is curved on one edge and tipped with tungsten carbide. There are various weights – you should find one that is comfortable for you but that is in proportion with the hardie (bolster blade).

3. Mouth and nose filter masks Wear these when cutting tesserae, mixing grout and cement or using strong smelling solvents.

4. Mosaic nippers These are used to cut vitreous glass, porcelain and ceramic tesserae. The cutting edge is tipped with tungsten carbide for durability. Buy nippers with spring action handles to make cutting less arduous.

5. Tile cutters These cutters carve through tiles in a two-step process. On one part of the cutters is a small wheel or blade and on the other, a flat edge known as the snapper. First the tile is scored with the blade and then 'snapped' with the flat edge.

6. Electric drill This is used for fixing mosaic projects. Buy a selection of rawl plugs and screws and invest in a countersink bit, which hides screw heads. A jigsaw is also a useful tool for delicate, intricate cutting.

7. Gummed brown paper or brown paper One side of the former type is gummed, which, when damp, will bond tesserae temporarily making it ideal for the indirect method (see page 7). If you use brown paper, apply gum glue to the shiny side.

8. Wood Used as a base material or support, the type of wood you use will depend on the weight and size of your mosaic, and whether it will be featured indoors or outside. Always prime before use.

9. Paintbrush/glue spreaders These are to paint and prime surfaces.

10. Polyvinyl acetate (PVA) glue This is excellent for priming or preparing surfaces.

11. Tape measure/ruler Measuring tools.

12. Spirit level This has a liquid measure and, when the bubble is central, the surface measured is straight. Check surfaces are straight before mosaicing directly onto the walls.

13. Safety glasses Wear these when cutting tesserae as slivers can damage your eyes.

14. Scissors Cutting tool for paper/card.

15. Gum glue This is a water-based adhesive. It is normally used with brown paper in the indirect method (see page 7).

16. Tweezers These are wonderful for picking up small tesserae and placing them in position or for pricking out unwanted pieces.

17. Bradawl This makes an excellent 'prodder' or pricking-out implement, which removes unwanted cement and mosaics.

18. Stanley knife Cutting tool for paper/card.

19. String Useful for creating large circles.

20. Masking tape This is not as sticky as adhesive tape and so is ideal for attaching the template to tracing paper temporarily.

21. Graph paper and sketch pad These are especially useful during the design stages.

22. Markers, pens and pencils Use markers to draw your design on the base of the mosaic. Pens and pencils are essential throughout.

SAFETY ADVICE

When cutting:
- wear surgical gloves, safety glasses, mouth and nose filters
- wear closed-toe shoes
- lay dust sheets if working indoors

When applying adhesives, grouts or sealants:
- follow manufacturers' instructions
- wear surgical or rubber gloves
- work in well-ventilated areas and use mouth and nose filters
- wear an apron or overalls
- lay dust sheets

When drilling:
- always unplug when changing bits
- wear safety glasses

CUTTING AND SCORING

MOSAIC NIPPERS: These are used to cut vitreous glass and porcelain tesserae. Hold the nippers in one hand and the tesserae in the other. Before cutting, get used to handling the nippers, which should be held towards the bottom of the handles. Place the tesserae face up in between the cutting edges of the nippers and then apply firm pressure.

Cutting in half Place the tessera halfway into the mosaic nippers. Squeeze the handles firmly and the tessera will break in half. If you need quarters, take half a tessera and repeat the procedure. The quarters can also be cut in half to create smaller tesserae that are ideal for outlining.

Cutting diagonals Place the tessera diagonally into the cutting edges of the nippers. Apply pressure and the piece should cut forming two triangles.

Cutting curves or circles This shape is slightly more fiddly to perfect than halves or diagonals, but can be achieved if you nip off each of the corners of the tessera. Then slowly 'nibble' all the way around the tile in order to produce a smooth round circular or oval shape.

HAMMER AND HARDIE (BOLSTER BLADE): Used to cut smalti and marble, this is similar to a tool used by the Romans. Make sure that your cutting hand is not restricted and be patient – perfect results take time.

TILE CUTTERS: These are useful if you want to cut ceramic tiles that measure more than 2.5cm square (1in square) and are ideal if you are using spare tiles left over from the bathroom or kitchen. They have a dual function: first, the cutter blade scores a line along the tile and then the snappers break it. For ceramic squares, cut strips and then score and snap them into squares. You can get larger cutters or cutting machines for cutting thicker tougher tiles.

Hammer and hardie (bolster blade) Position the tessera with your thumb and finger over the blade of the hardie where you want the cut to be. Bring the hammer down lightly and firmly onto the centre of the tessera. Avoid inhaling dust by standing back as you cut.

Scoring tiles In order to produce a scored line on your ceramic tile, place a metal rule in the exact position that you want the desired cutting line. Then run the tile cutter's blade along the metal rule applying even pressure as you go.

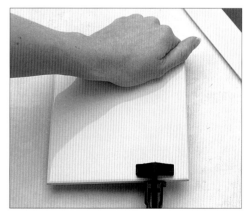

Snapping tiles Put the tile cutter's mouth over the centre of the scored line. Use your other hand to take the pressure away from the cut. Apply firm pressure to the cutters until you hear a 'snapping' noise when the tile is cut.

ADHESIVES, GROUTS AND TOOLS

There are different types of adhesives and grouts available but it is important that you choose the correct one for your project's requirements.

1. Polyvinyl acetate (PVA) glue (illustrated on page 3) A white glue that comes in two forms: water soluble and non-water soluble. The former can be used in the indirect method (see page 6). Also used to prime surfaces.

2. Gum glue (illustrated on page 3) This is usually water soluble and is used for the indirect method (see page 6).

3. Cement-based adhesives These are available in powder, ready-mixed or rapid setting forms. Using an additive will allow more movement and flexibility.

4. Mortar mix (not illustrated) Made from sand, cement and water, this is ideal for making an exterior floor mosaic. The ratio is generally 3:1, sharp sand to cement.

5. Grout Used to fill the gaps between the tesserae, this comes in ready-mixed or powder form and a variety of colours. Illustrated here is the cement-based powder form. Ready-made products are also available but they tend to leave a residue behind.

6. Epoxy Grout (not illustrated) This is a two-part resin-based grout, which creates a waterproof barrier.

7. Paint Scraper This can be used to apply small amounts of adhesive and grout.

8. Notched trowel This is used for laying the cement and it has a serrated or notched edge that combs the bed of cement, ensuring an even layer and creating a good key. A 3mm (⅛in) notched trowel is recommended for mosaics as it creates a smaller grooved bed.

9. Trowel Use a pointed-head trowel for applying cement in awkward areas, and for measuring and mixing adhesive and grouts.

10. Margin trowel Square-headed trowel.

11. Palette knives Available in different shaped heads, this is a flexible tool that is great for applying adhesive or grout in small areas and to smooth and remove excess.

12. Protective gloves Use rubber gloves when cleaning and grouting and surgical gloves when applying adhesive and cutting tesserae.

13. Grout float Used for applying grout, especially on larger projects, it also removes grout residue. Use a squeegee as an alternative.

14. Cloth Use for polishing grout residue.

15. Tiler's sponge Ideal for removing grout and cleaning. Use the sponge in circular movements to ensure an even coverage.

16. Sealants A wide variety of sealants are available – seek advice from a tile supplier for the product most suited to your project.

17. Additive for adhesive This is used with powdered adhesive and allows more natural movement. It is especially important when working on wood and floorboards.

18. Additive for grout This is used with the powdered grout and allows for flexibility. Read the label for safety advice.

19. Measuring jug This is used when measuring ratios of water, grout and glue.

MIXING CEMENT AND GROUT

Measuring ingredients Follow the manufacturers' instructions with regard to quantities and ratios of ingredients – you can use various measuring devices, such as one full trowel or one full measuring jug to represent one unit of material.

Adding water Pour the ingredients into a clean bucket. Slowly add water and additive, and mix with a trowel.

Smoothing the mixture Using a small trowel, mix the ingredients thoroughly. The texture should be quite smooth and free of lumps, neither too runny nor too thick.

DIRECT MOSAIC-LAYING METHOD

 Employing this method means that you apply the tesserae 'directly' in situ; that is, face up and one at a time straight onto the surface. The benefit of this technique is that you can see the work progress piece by piece. It is used in three-dimensional projects, on uneven surfaces, or in murals and splashbacks. The direct method is not recommended for flat surfaces as the results may be irregular.

1 Using abrasive paper and a block, remove the rough edges from the chosen base – here, a piece of wood. Run over the face of the base to create a good key.

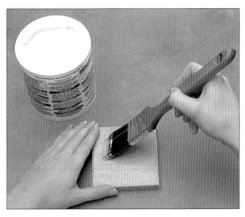

2 Paint the front and side edges with one coat of PVA glue to prime the surface. Make sure you clean your brush immediately after use, or it will become stiff.

3 While waiting for the glue to dry, prepare the adhesive and soak the mosaic pieces to free them from the brown paper backing. Once the PVA has dried completely, draw on your design with a pencil or marker pen.

4 Spread a small amount of adhesive onto the board and position the mosaic piece by piece, following your pencil design. Leave to dry for 24 hours. Wear gloves to protect your hands from the adhesive.

5 Clean your panel with a damp sponge then prick out excess cement with a bradawl or similar tool so that it will not show through the grout. If using marble tesserae, apply a protective coating.

6 Put on rubber gloves and mix a quantity of grout (see page 5). For small projects use a paint scraper, as shown, to squeeze the grout into the gaps between the tiles. Use a grout float or squeegee for larger projects.

7 After completely grouting the finished piece, remove the excess grout using a clean, damp sponge. Repeat this process several times and rinse your sponge regularly to keep it clean and avoid smearing.

8 Use a cloth to polish the surface, removing any residue. Leave the grout to dry for 24 hours and then apply a sealant to marble or porcelain tiles with a paintbrush or cloth, to protect them from staining.

INDIRECT MOSAIC-LAYING METHOD

This method is 'indirect' in the sense that you first lay out the mosaic on gummed brown paper, before pressing the entire finished design onto your chosen base. The indirect method is best used for larger projects, such as floors, so you can achieve a uniform flat surface. It is also better for areas that are not easily accessible.

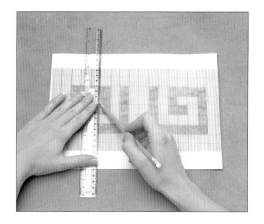

1 Draw your design and then trace onto tracing paper. Turn it over and transfer onto gummed paper (sticky side up) or brown paper, showing the design in reverse.

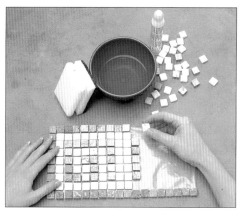

2 Stick the tesserae in position face down on the paper. For gummed paper use water for bonding; for brown paper use a water-soluble glue, such as gum glue.

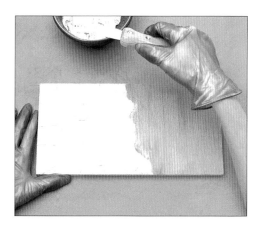

3 Prime your surface with PVA glue using a paintbrush. Prepare your adhesive-based cement (see page 5) and apply it to the base using a paint scraper or a trowel for larger projects. Wear gloves to protect your hands.

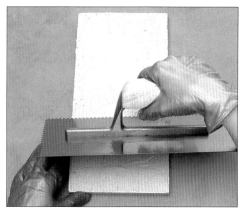

4 Drag a notched trowel at a 45-degree angle towards you in one sweeping action. This creates a grooved surface in the adhesive, which provides a good key in which the tesserae can bond.

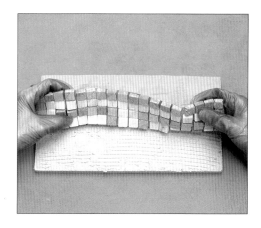

5 Carefully lift the mosaic and line its top edge with the top of the wood. Slowly lower the mosaic onto the adhesive bed. Smooth and press the tesserae with your hands. Leave to dry for 24 hours.

6 Moisten the paper with a wet sponge and peel it off to reveal the design. If any tesserae are attached to the paper, stick them down again with more adhesive and leave to dry. Prick out excess cement with a bradawl.

7 Wearing rubber gloves, prepare and apply the grout, pushing it into the gaps. Remove any excess with a damp sponge, rinsing the sponge frequently to avoid simply smearing rather than removing the grout.

8 Polish the mosaic with a cloth to remove the fine layer of grout residue. Leave to dry for 24 hours and then polish once again. For marble mosaics you will need to apply a coat of sealant using a cloth or paintbrush.

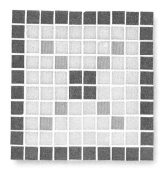

Greek Key Design Bathmat

TOOLS AND MATERIALS

2 x 2cm (¾ x ¾in) glass tesserae
Exterior MDF 84 x 39.5cm and
2.5cm thick (33 x 15in and1in
thick)
Waterproof PVA
Paintbrush
Brown paper
Pencil and ruler
Surgical and rubber gloves
Mask
PVA craft glue
Fine paintbrush
Two buckets for mixing
White exterior adhesive powder
White exterior grout powder
Notched trowel
Palette knife
Sponge
Bradawl or prodding tool

GLASS TESSERAE COLOURS

Deep aqua – 20.50 (1) (EU)
Mid aqua – 20.24 (1) (EU)
Pale aqua – 20.84 (1) (EU)
(See page 32 for key to suppliers)

The key motif is one of the most instantly recognizable Greek designs. Its simple, repeating pattern runs in a continuous, seemingly endless line. The key was typically used as an edging for elaborate designs on pottery and chiselled into sculptures as well as featuring as a detail on clothing and jewellery. Throughout ancient and modern Greece, it appears widely – on ornaments in the home, on the surrounding magnificent architecture and even as a linear border on traditional Greek costumes. This project is simple to make because there is no cutting of the tesserae involved and the indirect method is used to apply them to the wooden base of the bathmat. The combination of pale blues and aqua sets the scene for a peaceful, tranquil refuge in your bathroom.

USING THE TEMPLATE

Detach the template from the back of the book. Turn the tracing over and go over the outline on the reverse in pencil. Turn the tracing back over and position it on your brown paper. Trace over the front, transferring the design onto the brown paper. For this particular design, it helps to shade in the pattern so you can see clearly where the tesserae should be positioned. They are applied using the indirect method (see page 7 for instructions).

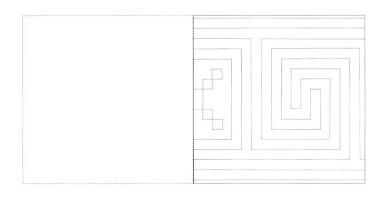

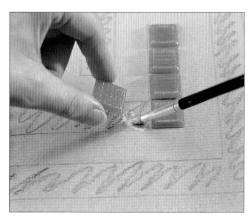

1 First paint the front, back and sides of the wood with two coats of waterproof PVA to seal it. This is essential if you are going to use the mat in a bathroom or it will eventually absorb water, expand and start to disintegrate, even if you have used exterior grade wood.

2 Draw over the lines of the template with a pencil and then flip it over and repeat the process onto the brown paper. You will now have a faint linear image on the brown paper. Using a pencil, shade in the pattern so that it will be easy to position the tesserae.

3 Stick the tiles in place right side down following the pattern. You can use gummed paper, applying water to make the tesserae stick, or use brown craft paper and diluted PVA adhesive. Try to keep the gaps between each tile equal so the grout will look regular and even.

5 Apply adhesive to the wood using a notched trowel and gently lower each half of the design into place. Next, using a small trowel apply adhesive onto the backs of the darkest tesserae and stick them one by one onto the edges of the board, being careful not to disturb the pattern.

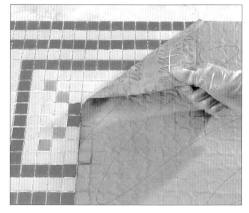

4 Now fill in the background colour so the design is complete and you are ready to stick the tiles to the wood. Turn the paper over and scribble a few lines running across the back. This may seem an odd thing to do but you are now going to cut the pattern in half with a craft knife so you have two smaller sections that will be easier to manoeuvre, and the lines you have scribbled will make registration much more efficient.

6 Leave it to dry for 24 hours. Wet the brown paper with a damp sponge and wait for it to soak in. The paper should peel off easily in two sections. If any tiles come loose, stick them down again.

7 Wait for the adhesive to dry. Some of it might seep through and stick out above the tiles. Using a bradawl pick out the excess and dust away the dry adhesive. Once this is done you are ready to grout.

HINTS AND TIPS

▶ If this is your first attempt, it might help to draw a rough sketch of the grid to help you position the tiles.

▶ Don't try to peel off the paper too soon – it takes longer than you might think.

▶ You may want to stick on rubber feet to raise the bathmat off the ground slightly so that water has less chance to seep in.

▶ You could use a wooden 'hockey stick' moulding as edging rather than using tiles.

8 Mix up the grout and spread it over the whole mosaic. Disperse it with a squeegee or trowel and work it into the gaps. Use your fingers to neaten the grout round the outside of the design. You may need to wait for the outside edges to dry and regrout to get a good edge. Polish the mosaic with a cloth and the project is complete.

INSPIRATIONAL IDEAS

By using quarter tiles you can shrink the design to make a pretty dado border, a border running along the top of a skirting board or an attractive surround for a mirror.

Garden Stepping Stones

TOOLS AND MATERIALS

18 x 18mm (¾ x ¾in) ceramic
tesserae
Concrete garden slabs
30cm x 30cm (12 x 12in)
Brown paper
Pencil
Craft knife
PVA glue
Fine paintbrush
Sponge
Concrete sealer and brush
Two buckets for mixing
Grey exterior adhesive powder
Grey exterior grout powder
Surgical gloves and rubber gloves
Mask and goggles
Score and snap nippers
Mosaic nippers
Trowel
Notched trowel
Cloth

CERAMIC TESSERAE COLOURS

Dark blue *(EU)*
Black *(EU)*
White *(EU)*
(See page 32 for key to suppliers)

This is a simple yet effective project that does not take long to complete. It is extremely satisfying to make because it looks deceptively complex. The stones are decorated with three geometric designs that are translated into six different patterns by reversing the colour schemes. There is some cutting involved but the pieces do not have to be perfectly even so it is not difficult. Muted tones of dusky blue, black and chalky white are used to create a harmonious classical effect. In some villages on the Greek islands, these patterns are used to decorate the outside of houses. The islanders mix and match a variety of designs but with a very limited palette, sometimes only two colours, to create greater impact. Despite the antiquity of the designs, the finished result looks stylish and modern.

USING THE TEMPLATE

Detach the template from the back of the book. Note that the designs on the template only show half of each pattern. Turn the tracing over and go over the outline on the reverse in pencil. Turn the tracing back over and position it on your brown paper. Trace over the front, transferring a copy of each half design onto the brown paper. Then flip the template over and trace each design again. Each slab requires two halves of the design so you will have to match up the two halves to make the complete pattern for each stone.

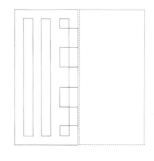 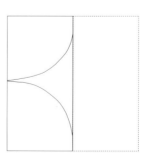 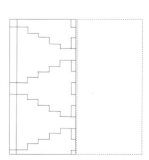

1 Seal all the stabs with a concrete sealer. This is usually white when you apply it and gets clearer when it is dry, like PVA. Choose the flattest slabs you can but if they are a bit uneven, you can even them out when you apply the adhesive.

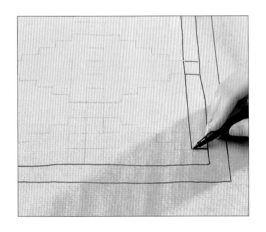

2 Trace two copies of each design onto pieces of brown paper. The template only shows half of the pattern; to create the whole pattern for each slab, trace the template once then flip it over and trace again, two halves for each slab.

3 Stick all the whole tiles onto the brown paper using diluted PVA adhesive. Score and snap rectangles to fill in the sections that are too small to fit whole tiles on the star-patterned stone. Make the shapes you need by holding the tesserae and nipping them a third of the way down on an angle so you get irregular pieces. Make sure you follow the advice on cutting given on page 4.

4 When all the tiles are stuck down in place forming the pattern, trim the edges of the brown paper with a craft knife. This makes it easier to position the tiles on your slabs and ensure that the mosaic is neatly lined up at the edges.

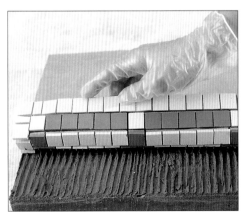

5 Cover the slabs with adhesive using a notched trowel and gently lower each piece of paper onto them, tile side down. Push the design gently into the adhesive, making sure they are embedded well enough to stick.

HINTS AND TIPS

▶ If the slabs are chipped it is a good idea to level them out with a bit of adhesive and leave this to dry completely before you get to step 5 in the project.

▶ The grout might not get into all the gaps and holes may appear while you are working; if so, simply rub grout into the holes to fill them up.

▶ When you are pressing the tesserae on their brown paper backing into the adhesive, remember that you are not trying to fill in the gaps between the tesserae, but make sure the tiles are embedded well enough in the adhesive for them to stick.

▶ Clean tools used for applying adhesive and grouting immediately after use.

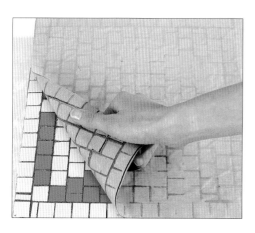

6 Leave the slabs overnight to dry. Dampen the paper with water and wait for it to come loose. Gently peel back each piece till all six patterns are revealed. Stick down any tesserae that come loose.

7 Using a bradawl, pick out any adhesive that has squeezed its way through to the surface and dust away the powder. Be meticulous as your adhesive and grout might vary in colour and it will show later.

8 Mix up enough grout for all the tiles and trowel it into the gaps. The edges of the slabs may be uneven or a different colour so for a more professional look, you should grout the edges of the tiles.

9 Wipe off any excess grout and polish the tiles to reveal the true colours of the tesserae. All that remains is to lower the slabs into the positions you want them in your garden.

INSPIRATIONAL IDEAS

Try changing the colours used for this design to earth tones – rich terracottas and warm ochres – to give a rustic feel.

You could use half of the template and repeat it to create an attractive edging border rather than flipping it over to create a square. Or use one design repeated over and over to create a border or stripe down a garden path.

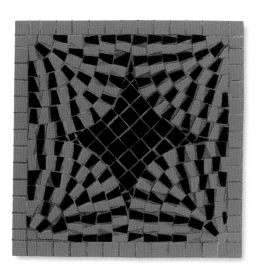

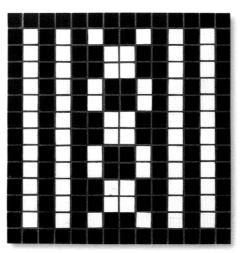

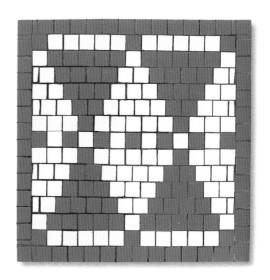

Rustic Fish Tablemat

TOOLS AND MATERIALS

Exterior MDF 57 x 37.5cm and
2.5cm thick (22 x 15in and 1in
thick)
Waterproof PVA
Paintbrush
Brown paper
Pencil
PVA
Fine paintbrush
Permanent marker
2 x 2 cm (¾ x ¾in) glass tesserae
Mirror tesserae
Two buckets
Trowel
Notched trowel
White exterior adhesive powder
White external grout powder
Safety goggles and mask
Sponge and squeegee
Cloth
Tile nippers
Tile score and snap nippers
Bradawl

GLASS TESSERAE COLOURS

White – 20.10 (1) (EU)
Dark blue – 20.46 (2) (EU)
Mid blue – 20.64 (2) (EU)
Mirror tesserae (craft shops)
(See page 32 for key to suppliers)

The sea features strongly in the myths and legends of ancient Greece and it has always been at the centre of Greek culture. So much of Greece and its islands are surrounded by water that ships, fish and all thing aquatic have had a huge influence on their designs for all kinds of everyday objects. Many of the houses are white-washed and stand in stark contrast with the blue Mediterranean sky and sea, forming the typical Greek colour palette. This project combines the white and blue colour scheme with a fish design highlighted with mirror tesserae. The project can be tackled in many ways: the shapes of tesserae used to fill the design are only a suggestion, and you could use any shapes you like. The tesserae are applied to your wood using the indirect method then a border is stuck down by the direct method.

USING THE TEMPLATE

Detach the template from the back of the book. Turn the tracing over and go over the outline on the reverse in pencil. Turn the tracing back over and position it on your brown paper. Trace over the front, transferring the design onto the brown paper. You may wish to go over this outline again in permanent marker pen to make sure it is clearly visible when you come to stick down the tesserae.

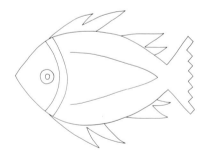

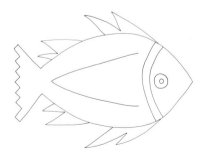

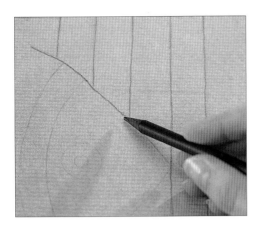

1 Trace the template onto the matt side of brown paper then go over the pencil line with permanent marker. The pencil line always seems a bit too faint and you can work more quickly with a clearer design.

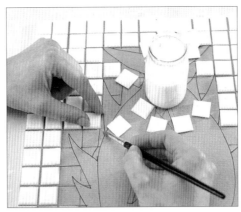

2 Stick down all the whole white tiles that require no cutting first. It can be easier to draw a squared grid for the white tiles so that you can position them quickly and accurately.

3 Cut lots of half tesserae and nip them into squares ready for the body of the fish. Next nibble a square into a tiny circle to form the eye. Read the advice about cutting on page 4 before you start.

4 Cutting the mirror tiles is easier than you would think. All you have to do is score them and then snap. Cut them into halves and squares and then little rectangles to go round the fishes' eyes.

5 Fill in the eye of the fish first and then the rest of the head. Insert a line of silver mirror tesserae to add shimmer and shine to the finished project.

6 When you get to the fin section, sketch the pattern you want first. You may choose to simplify the shapes or perhaps you would like to add more silver. Press the tesserae down firmly on your brown paper. If you cannot find gummed paper, you can use brown craft paper with diluted PVA glue to stick the tesserae down.

7 Finish all the blue and silver areas then start to fill in the white tiles nipping off sections to fit the holes. Leave all this to dry and trim the edges of the paper ready to stick it to the wood.

8 Seal the wood with waterproof PVA then apply the adhesive with a notched trowel. Gently lower the fishes into place and push the panel into the adhesive.

9 Carefully stick individual tiles around the outside to form a neat edge, buttering each tile with adhesive and holding it in place for a few seconds.

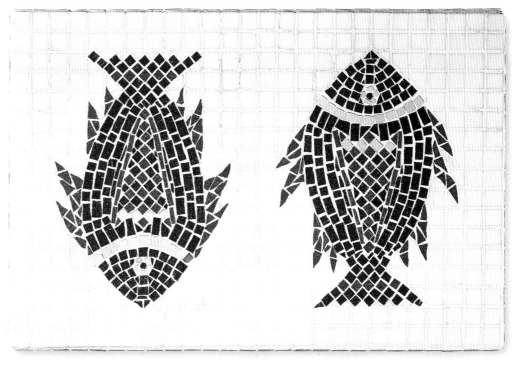

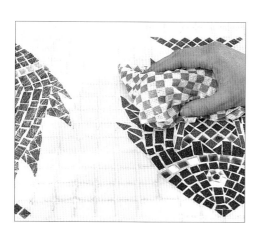

10 When it has dried, soak off the brown paper, pick out excess adhesive, grout and polish.

HINTS AND TIPS

▶ Try out different combination of patterns and colours on paper first to help you decide the effect you want.

▶ It might be a good idea to back the mosaic with sticky-back felt or rubber feet to prevent it from scratching the tabletop or other surface you plan to use it on.

INSPIRATIONAL IDEAS

The fish design would also look wonderful in a bathroom, swimming on the wall round a bath, or as a splashback behind a basin. See pages 20 to 23 for instructions on how to make a wall frieze.

Seahorse Wall Frieze

TOOLS AND MATERIALS

2 x 2cm (¾ x ¾in) glass tesserae
Pencil
Masking tape
Waterproof PVA
Paintbrush
Spirit level
Tape measure
White exterior adhesive powder
White exterior grout powder
Goggles and mask
Two buckets
Trowel
Sponge
Cloth
Tile nippers
Surgical gloves and rubber gloves

GLASS TES0 COLOURS

Sea green – 20.57 (2) (EU)
Pale aqua – 20.35 (2) (EU)
Dark sea green – 20.67 (2) (EU)
Leaf green – 20.39 (2) (EU)
Grass green – 20.72 (2) (EU)
(See page 32 for key to suppliers)

G reek mythology is steeped in fantastic stories about sea creatures, and they are replicated in many classical mosaics. Tiny seahorses are among the most charming marine animals and this project combines waves of seahorses with an interlinking chain design. The chain is traditionally used in Greek art and architecture, as part of a larger design, to create a border or just in its own right. This project is simpler than it may at first appear. The majority of the tesserae are whole or just have their edges nipped off. The only real cutting and detail is in the seahorses. The tesserae are applied using the direct method. This versatile design would look stunning in the garden, as we have used it here, or running around a bathroom wall as a dado border.

USING THE TEMPLATE

Detach the template from the back of the book. Turn the tracing over and go over the outline on the reverse in pencil. Turn the tracing back over and position it on your wall. Trace over the front, transferring the design onto the wall. You may wish to go over this outline again in permanent marker pen to make sure it is clearly visible when you come to stick down the tesserae. Repeat the tracing to fill the length of wall that you want the frieze to run along.

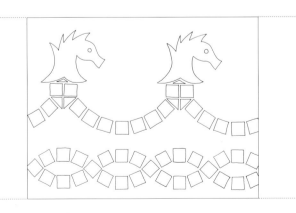

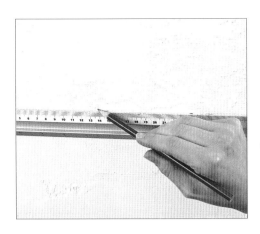

1 Draw parallel lines in pencil on your wall in the position where you want your frieze to run, 30.5cm (12in) apart. Use a tape measure and spirit level to ensure that your lines are completely straight.

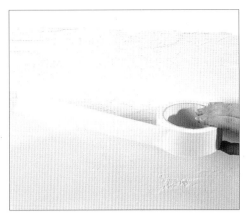

2 Stick masking tape along the top edge of the top line and along the bottom of the bottom line. These are your guidelines for the whole project and will make sticking and grouting much easier.

3 Choose the direction you want the seahorses to face and trace the design onto the wall. You may want to go over the lines freehand with a marker pen so you can see them better.

4 Start with the lines between the seahorses and the linking chains, which only use whole tiles. Mix up white adhesive and spread it on each tesserae then press them down one by one.

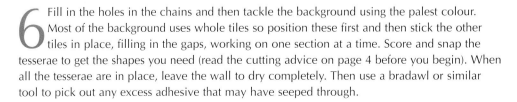

5 Cut heaps of half tiles, quarters, triangles and little rectangles to work on the seahorses. Cut the eye shapes by nibbling a quarter into a circle. Work your way from the nose up the head and then down from the mane to the neck.

6 Fill in the holes in the chains and then tackle the background using the palest colour. Most of the background uses whole tiles so position these first and then stick the other tiles in place, filling in the gaps, working on one section at a time. Score and snap the tesserae to get the shapes you need (read the cutting advice on page 4 before you begin). When all the tesserae are in place, leave the wall to dry completely. Then use a bradawl or similar tool to pick out any excess adhesive that may have seeped through.

7 Mix up the grout and cover the whole surface between the masking tape tramlines. The grout needs to be quite solid so it does not slide down the walls.

8 Wipe off the excess grout with a cloth and polish the mosaic to bring out the true colours. Peel off the masking tape from above and below and your frieze is complete.

INSPIRATIONAL IDEAS

You could use this linking border around anything. Try it surrounding a garden

water feature such as a fountain or fish pond.

For a really authentic Greek appearance, you could have white seahorses with

a Mediterranean blue background, which looks simple yet striking. Or use

metallic tesserae to make the pattern glisten.

HINTS AND TIPS

▶ For the seahorses' manes, nip whole tesserae into halves and nip them again on the diagonal creating triangles.

▶ If the masking tape gets covered in adhesive, peel it off and replace it to make a neater edge when grouting.

▶ You may need to touch up the edges with paint, so it would be useful if you have some left over from when you last painted the wall.

Olive Branch Mirror

TOOLS AND MATERIALS

23 x 23mm (⁹⁄₁₀ x ⁹⁄₁₀in) ceramic tesserae
Two pieces of MDF cut 60 x 60cm and 12mm thick (24 x 24in and ½in thick)
Jigsaw to cut the circles
Mirror to fit the hole
PVA
Paintbrush
Pencil, string and nail
Tape measure
Workbench
Cramps
Mosaic nippers
White adhesive powder
Beige grout powder
Goggles and mask
Trowel
Palette knife
Gloves
Two buckets

CERAMIC TESSERAE COLOURS

Brown – *138 (RH)*
Green – *215 (RH)*
Blue – *116 (RH)*
Red – *133 (RH)*
White – *200 (RH)*
(See page 32 for key to suppliers)

Greece is renowned for its abundance of olive trees and excellent olive oil. Olives are a symbol of hope, peace and general wellbeing so they are a natural choice for a Greek mosaic project. The gently curving branches in olive green, highlighted with blue leaves and plump, chocolate-coloured olives, combine to create a warm Mediterranean feel. The mirror will make a beautiful feature for hallways or living rooms, bathrooms or bedrooms. This project is quite time-consuming but you will soon work out how to cut all the odd-shaped pieces you need. You can either cut each tile to fit a specific place or just cut heaps and move them around like a jigsaw puzzle until you find a place where each fits. Don't throw away any off-cuts as there is bound to be a place for them.

USING THE TEMPLATE

Detach the template from the back of the book. Turn the tracing over and go over the outline on the reverse in pencil. Turn the tracing back over and position it on your frame. Trace over the front, transferring the design onto the frame. The template only shows half of the design so you will have to flip it over, re-pencil it and repeat the tracing to complete the circle, joining the edges carefully so the pattern appears seamless.

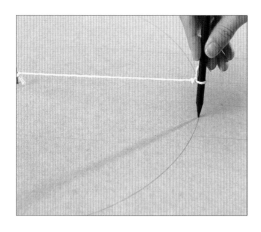

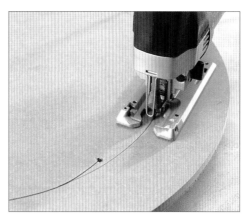

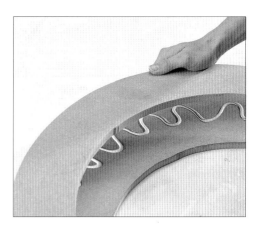

1 Draw a circle with a diameter of 59cm (23in) on each piece of wood, using a length of string, a nail and a pencil to construct a basic compass (see Hints and Tips). On the first circle, draw another line 11cm (4in) in from the edge. This is the front.

2 On the second circle, draw a line 5cm (2in) in from the edge. This is the back. Cut round the outsides of the bigger circles, then drill a hole large enough to fit the drillbit on the inside of the lines. Guide the jigsaw round till you have two rings.

3 Liberally apply wood glue to one of the rings and then clamp them together and leave to dry. When they are totally dry, cover the whole frame back and front with PVA adhesive to seal the wood. Wash your brush immediately after use.

5 To cut out the olives, take a tessera and nip it in half with your mosaic nippers. Nip again into quarters and then nibble the edges till you have little round shapes.

4 Trace the design from the template onto the front of the frame. The template only shows half the design so once you have completed one side, flip over the template, re-pencil it and repeat the tracing. If you flip the tracing and do not re-pencil, your branches will face in different directions. Either way looks good. The choice is yours.

6 To make the leaves, cut tiles in half and then at an angle cut triangles. Mix up some adhesive and stick all the leaves, stalks and olives in place a section at a time and leave them to dry.

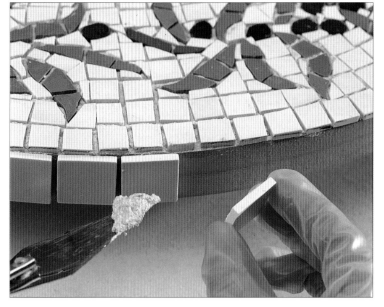

7 Fill in the background lines with as many quarter tiles as possible, then fill in the gaps. Butter the backs of the tesserae with adhesive and stick whole tiles round the outside edge and quarter tiles on the inside edge. Leave to dry for 24 hours.

8 Prick out any excess adhesive with a bradawl and wipe away any dust. Then apply beige grout. Wipe off the excess with a squeegee and polish with a clean cloth. Use a slightly damp cloth for the first clean and a dry one for the second.

HINTS AND TIPS

▶ To draw the circles on your pieces of wood, mark the centre of the wood with a dot and tie your pencil onto the end of the string. Attach a nail to the string 29.5cm (11½in) from the pencil and gently tap the nail into the centre dot. Hold the string taut and draw the circles, keeping your pencil upright on the wood.

▶ When you fill in the background, start with the edges and work your way in. That way you can use as many whole quarters as possible. The rest of the background is made up of nibbled quarters and chipped off-cuts.

▶ To make the stalk pieces, cut a red tessera in half and then cut it again lengthways. It should split unevenly, just as you want it. If you find this hard, score and snap the lines.

INSPIRATIONAL IDEAS

This design would look great as a border in a

shower or along the back of your kitchen units.

You could make a square mirror instead, with

each side using two branches that face in

opposite directions.

Leaf and Lotus Flower Table

TOOLS AND MATERIALS

2 x 2cm (¾ x ¾in) glass tesserae
Metal table base
Exterior MDF 80 x 80cm
(31½ x 31½in); depth will depend
on the base
Waterproof PVA
Paintbrush
Two buckets
Palette knife
Trowel
Exterior white powder adhesive
Exterior white grout powder
Goggles and mask
Gloves
Sponge squeegee
Cloth

GLASS TESSERAE COLOURS

Dark green – *20.67 (2) (EU)*
Turquoise – *20.50 (1) (EU)*
Ice blue – *20.22 (1) (EU)*
Cool white – *20.09 (1) (EU)*
(See page 32 for key to suppliers)

The attractive pattern of Palmette-and-Lotus was traditionally used to decorate all kinds of everyday objects in the Greek household. Palmette is a group of simple leaves arranged in a fan shape, resembling a palm tree leaf; here it is combined with a lotus flower and linking tendrils to form a stunning overall design. This project is a simplified version of an authentic pattern, using calm, fluid tones of green, turquoise and ice blue against an off-white background. Applying ivory grout to the mottled white tesserae background gives the tabletop a rustic feel. The pattern itself is easy to complete as most of it uses half or quarter tesserae, and they are applied using the direct method. The finished table would look wonderful in a conservatory or outdoors on a patio in summer.

USING THE TEMPLATE

Detach the template from the back of the book. Turn the tracing over and go over the outline on the reverse in pencil. Turn the tracing back over and position it on your wood. Trace over the front, transferring the design onto the wood. The template only shows a quarter of the design so you will have to flip it over, re-pencil it and repeat the tracing four times to complete the circle, matching up the pattern carefully.

1 To fit our table base, we drew a circle of 80cm (31½in) diameter on exterior MDF and cut it out with a jigsaw. Then seal the wood with waterproof PVA adhesive on both sides and around the edges.

2 Draw on the back of the template with a pencil. Turn it over and position it on one quarter of the table. Trace over the lines to transfer the design onto the wood.

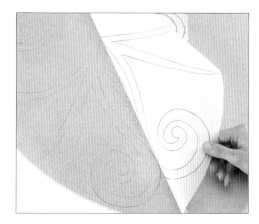

3 Flip the template over and reposition it, butting up to the pencil lines you have just marked. Repeat the process four times and you will have formed a circle.

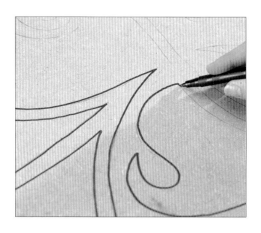

4 The lines do not always show up on PVA-coated wood, so it is a good idea to go over them freehand with a permanent marker so you can see them clearly when you come to position the tesserae.

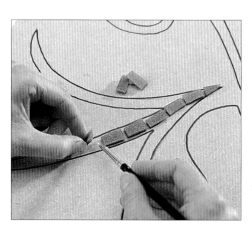

5 Cut heaps of the green tesserae into halves and proceed from the centre outwards, working systematically along each shape. Fill in the other areas with as many whole quarters as you can and then cut pieces to fit the rest.

6 While you are working, only mix the quantity of adhesive you need for each area so that it doesn't dry. The background is mainly covered in quarter tesserae. Cut plenty of these as you will use them up quickly. Work along each shape with sweeping lines so the background has a rhythm. This project will take quite a few sittings to complete but it is very satisfying to see the pattern emerging. When you have finished, leave the mosaic to dry completely.

7 Mix up beige grout and smear it all over the table. Work it into all the gaps and right up to the edges so you have a smooth even surface.

INSPIRATIONAL IDEAS

This design would look equally good on a square tabletop. You could make the design in white reversed out of a blue and green background. You could try mosaicing a half circle and use it as a plaque above a doorway.

8 Wipe off all the excess grout and polish your table top with a clean cloth. Your table top is now ready to slot into your table base. We chose a base made of galvanized steel so that the table can be used outside.

HINTS AND TIPS

▶ When you work on the turquoise leaf patterns, go from the inside of the table outwards. Stick the tesserae in lines as far as you can. For example, on the long leaves stick a row in the middle first and then up the sides, then fill in the gaps.

▶ Try to end up with a row of whole quarters on the outside border. This gives the table a nice neat edge.

▶ Fill in the background one section at a time.

ACKNOWLEDGEMENTS

Thanks to Mum and Roy, Mia and Patrice Bouëdo, La Iguana Perdida, Kathy Fanshaw, Medallion Man, Louisa, Derek and Rose for the loan of their garden, Abby, Andy and Rose Lord, and especially Caroline, Graeme and The Feel Good Studios.

Thanks also to the following firms:

Edgar Udny & Co Ltd *[EU]*
314 Balham High Road
London SW17 7AA
Tel: 020 8767 8181
Fax: 020 8767 7709

Suppliers of vitreous glass, smalti, gold and silver leaf, as well as fixing materials and gummed brown paper. Mail order service available.

Reed Harris *[RH]*
Riverside House, 27 Carnwath Road
London SW6 3HR
Tel: 020 7736 7511
Fax: 020 7736 2988

Supplier of household tiles, porcelain and marble tesserae as well as sealants, tools, adhesives and grout. Mail order service available.

Paul Fricker Ltd
Well Park, Willeys Avenue
Exeter EX2 8BE
Tel: 01392 278636
Fax: 01392 410508

Specialists in glass tesserae and suppliers of all materials. Mail order service available.

Forged Frontiers
Devon Marketing
Ilsham Point
21 Bishops Close
Torquay, Devon TQ1 2PL

For table bases.

Mosaics are sold nationwide by branches of **B&Q**, **Fired Earth** and **Hobby Craft**.

In Australia, materials are available from tiling specialists and major hardware stores.

Published by Murdoch Books UK Ltd
First published in 2001

ISBN 1-85391-992 6
A catalogue record of this book is available from the British Library.
© Text, design, photography and illustrations Murdoch Books UK Ltd 2001.

Commissioning Editor: Natasha Martyn-Johns
Project Editor: Anna Nicholas
Designer: Cathy Layzell
Photographer: Graeme Ainscough
Stylist: Caroline Davis

CEO: Robert Oerton
Publisher: Catie Ziller
Publishing Manager: Fia Fornari
Production Manager: Lucy Byrne

Group General Manager: Mark Smith
Group CEO/Publisher: Anne Wilson

All rights reserved. No part of this publication may be reproduced, stored in a retrieval system, or transmitted in any form or by any means, electronic, mechanical, photocopying, recording or otherwise without the prior written permission of the publisher.

Colour separation by Colourscan, Singapore
Printed in Singapore by Imago

Murdoch Books UK Ltd
Ferry House, 51–57 Lacy Road,
Putney, London, SW15 1PR
Tel: +44 (0)20 8355 1480
Fax: +44 (0)20 83551499
Murdoch Books (UK) Ltd is a subsidiary of Murdoch Magazines Pty Ltd.

Murdoch Books®
GPO Box 1203
Sydney NSW 1045
Tel: +61 (0)20 9692 2347
Fax: +61 (0)20 9692 2559
Murdoch Books® is a trademark of Murdoch Magazines Pty Ltd.